The Brightwater Anthology
WRITERS CELEBRATE LIFE AROUND THE RIVER SKERNE

The Brightwater Anthology
WRITERS CELEBRATE LIFE AROUND
THE RIVER SKERNE

The Brightwater Anthology:

Writers Celebrate Life Around the River Skerne

This edition has been published in 2022
in the United Kingdom by Paper + Ink.

www.paperand.ink
Twitter: @paper_andink
Instagram: paper_and_ink

"Gold Rush" © Chrissie Robinson
"Outrunning" and "Plane Sailing: The Flight of the *Stormbird*" © Peter Barron
"Tipster" © Mark James Chappell
"The Great Tomato Train Rescue" and "Noble Behemoths of the Skerne:
South Durham's Cattle Chronicles " © Chris Lloyd
"Homecoming" © Michael Drew
"Our House" © Fran Edwards
"Wherever Went the River" © John Ridsdale

"Outrunning", "Plane Sailing: The Flight of the *Stormbird*",
"The Great Tomato Train Rescue" and "Noble Behemoths of the Skerne:
South Durham's Cattle Chronicles " have been published previously
in modified form in *The Northern Echo*.

Special thanks to Jessica Andrews,
who judged the Brightwater Short Story Competition 2022 shortlist.

1 2 3 4 5 6 7 8 9 10

ISBN 9781911475637

A CIP catalogue record for this book is available from the British Library.
Jacket design by James Nunn: www.jamesnunn.co.uk | @Gnunkse
Printed and bound in Great Britain.

CONTENTS

Introduction
Paul Black and Steve Gater

9

Gold Rush
Chrissie Robinson
FIRST-PRIZE WINNER OF THE BRIGHTWATER
SHORT STORY COMPETITION 2022

11

Outrunning
Peter Barron

21

Tipster
Mark James Chappell
RUNNER-UP, BRIGHTWATER
SHORT STORY COMPETITION 2022

27

CONTENTS

The Great Tomato Train Rescue
Chris Lloyd
33

Homecoming
Michael Drew
RUNNER-UP, BRIGHTWATER
SHORT STORY COMPETITION 2022
41

Plane Sailing: The Flight of the Stormbird
Peter Barron
57

Our House
Fran Edwards
RUNNER-UP, BRIGHTWATER
SHORT STORY COMPETITION 2022
63

Noble Behemoths of the Skerne: South Durham's Cattle Chronicles
Chris Lloyd
73

CONTENTS

Wherever Went the River
John Ridsdale
RUNNER-UP, BRIGHTWATER
SHORT STORY COMPETITION 2022
85

Author Biographies
113

INTRODUCTION

The River Skerne's name, we think, comes from an old Viking word meaning *bright* or *shining*.

The river still lives up to that in places.

At Hurworth Burn you can watch herons, swans and lapwings. At Ketton, you may catch a glimpse of an otter near the birthplace of the Durham Ox – one of a number of huge eighteenth-century cattle bred on the banks of the Skerne, providing the foundations for global cattle breeding and exports of the Durham shorthorn throughout the world.

Downstream, history has not been so kind; the river suffered from many of the innovations of the Industrial Revolution. In 1825, the Stockton and Darlington Railway Company, the world's first public railway company to use steam engines, was created by the likes of George Stephenson and the Quaker Pease family. These early pioneers

INTRODUCTION

also later exported their engineering and railway business know-how throughout the world.

Discover Brightwater (our take on the old Viking name) is one of the good causes that have been supported by all the people who play the National Lottery, via the National Lottery Heritage Fund. We've been funded to restore parts of the River Skerne and our ancient wetland habitats, and improve public footpaths. We've investigated our Roman and medieval history. And we've been helping to tell the story of the Skerne online, and through publications, music and events.

We are delighted to support this anthology, which, like Discover Brightwater itself, helps to restore, reveal and celebrate life around the River Skerne.

Paul Black, Programme Manager
Discover Brightwater

Steve Gater, Chair
Discover Brightwater Landscape Partnership

GOLD RUSH

CHRISSIE ROBINSON

Word trickled through the village just like its resident river. Of course, they didn't believe it at first – why would they? Little boys told untruths, embellished, hacked at realities … but this boy had evidence, balanced on the palm of a held-out hand. You couldn't argue with solid fact.

"It's a trick," snapped Alice.

"It ain't real," barked Bill.

And they ushered their grubby grandson to his room. "Go change, our Arlo; wash up for tea. It'll be ready by the time you're done."

Deflated, defeated, Arlo stomped up the stairs, doing as he was told but with fierce resentment, throwing his finds like dice, not watching where they rolled.

● ● ●

It looked the same, but felt different. Funny what a few months can do to a person. He remembered the last time he was here, fresh out of college and full of ideas. Unlike his mates, he had his life planned out – or, at least, the next chapter of it, any road.

He'd half expected to find them here, dossing by the Skerne, chucking sticks and chugging cans, no plans for this day or the next or the next.

He couldn't bring himself to sit on the sofa, the same one he had sat on many times before, had his own hand in bringing here after they'd found it in the alley off Salters Lane. He'd sat on it then. Sat on it with her. They hadn't thought about germs and vermin then, only love and White Lightning.

A shoe on dry kindling turned his head to the embankment. There she was, fresh from his mind and in the flesh.

"Loll, you came."

"What're you after, Si?"

GOLD RUSH

* * *

Alice switched the TV to standby, sighed and stood up, sick to the back teeth of depressing adverts reminding her of her mortality, telling her how close to death she was, urging her to get her affairs in order before she went.

Bill was at his weekly luncheon club and Arlo, well, Arlo had better be at school at least *attempting* to get a decent education, and not skiving down at that wretched river. She sighed a second time. She supposed she'd better get a wash in the machine, make good use of the afternoon's fair forecast.

Bill was better trained. He'd had more years at it. He still left crumbs on the kitchen counter and rarely washed the pots – but his laundry always reached the basket. Arlo, on the other hand, hadn't had that constant reprimand, never knew the word *no* until just a few weeks ago; but he'd learn, in time. Alice and Bill would make sure of that.

Meanwhile, his clothes piled in small mounds around his room like brightly coloured cowpats.

Alice began scooping them up, almost as cautiously as if they had actually come from an animal's behind. Well, you could never always tell what you might find in, or on, a boy's clothing. Or under, apparently: Alice's attention was drawn to the floor by a clatter. Something small, a pebble ... smaller. It was the size and shape of a chocolate raisin, but not brown. She picked it up, felt its weight, held it up for closer inspection, remembered what Arlo had said. Then she shook her head and placed it in the pocket of her floral pink pinny. She carried the clothes downstairs to the kitchen, filled the machine, set it away and took another look at the nugget in her pocket.

She held it up to the window, to the light, and caught sight of Jenny next door, who'd had the same idea about the weather and the washing, by the looks of it, but perhaps an hour or so sooner – she was already on pegging hers out on the line. Alice dashed out to catch her.

"Here, Jenny, take a look at this, love, and tell me what you think."

Jenny gave inspection. "Bit small, not worth much, I daresay."

"But it is ...?"

"Gold, aye, from what I can tell ... but if you want to know for sure, I'd say you want to go see Frederick up the shop. He's been dealing in that stuff for years. Well, in rings and things, but still."

"Thanks, Jenny." Alice turned to leave.

"Here, where'd you get it?"

"You'd never believe."

"Try me," Jenny goaded.

"The Skerne."

"Get away!"

Alice made to leave. She was away to see Frederick, just as Jenny had suggested.

"Wait up, Alice ... wait up!" Jenny was the perfect shadow, in the fact that she could keep up with Alice's quick pace. She wasn't as silent as a shadow, though, calling to everyone they passed: "Here, did you know, our Alice has found gold!"

Some dismissed her just as Arlo had been dismissed, but by the time Alice and Jenny arrived at Freddy's Treasure Trove, they had accumulated a small entourage. Everyone cooed at the news that gold had been found in the Skerne.

* * *

Si started with some easy openers, as if passing time of day with an almost-stranger. *How's you? How's your mam? What you been doing since you got home?*

Loll's answers were short on great detail.

Si moved on – or back, rather, to reminiscence. He talked about how they'd met that first day at school when the young villagers merged into one senior institution. How it took him ages to pluck up the courage to ask her out. The numerous evenings and weekends thereafter, spent together, quite often down here by the river. Then college, then their big adventure together when both applied to – and got – their first jobs on board the same ship on the entertainments team. Their first far-flung port of call: Cartagena, Colombia ... and now, back here.

He was done rambling. Loll hadn't gotten a word in, only the odd nod and brief noise. "I'm sorry," she offered. "I missed home, my mam, too much."

"And I missed you."

Loll had flown home after three months in. Si had stayed for the full nine-month contract and was now back for three months – or for good, depending on what happened next.

"The ship went back to Cartagena," he said. "I got us something from there." Si reached into his jacket pocket and pulled out a clear tube. "They sold them like this. I thought it would be a good idea, as you weren't there to pick your own." He took Loll's hand and gently peeled it open, palm side up, so she could cup the contents he spilled from the container. "We can get them melted. Any style we want. Matching bands. What do you think?"

Loll didn't move, didn't speak.

Si knelt down, his knee on dry dirt, finally getting to the question he had carried with him halfway across the world. "What do you say, Loll, Lolly, Lollypop … will you marry me?"

They came with colanders, skillets and sieves – men, women and kids, all dressed for brambling or tatty picking or fishing. The latter was the closest guess, but you'd be hard-pressed to find fish in this part of the Skerne. Tiddlers, maybe, but more likely just a quiver on the skin of the water, made by a boatman or swimmer or skipper.

Alice was there, front of line, then Bill, full of dinner, being dragged behind. Surely the claim was *theirs* to stake; it was, after all, their Arlo's discovery. But more claims came. There was the farmer, for one, who owned the land that the river wrapped around. Surely what's found was his! Then, of course, came the local councillor, with the "best interest of the community" at his heart. Gold found should be shared *with* the community, *for* the community ... that was his first and only thought.

News crews got wind and turned up in their vans, cameras on shoulders and microphones in hands. The Yukon, they compared it to, this little unassuming Durham vale, and once word got out, the outsiders arrived, non-locals trying to stick their fingers into pies that weren't theirs.

A few more nuggets, just as small as the first, were found over the coming days. Just enough to keep hope flickering.

*   *   *

Loll curls her fingers around the nuggets, places her fist over Si's open hand, releases them and him in one swift drop ... and with no explanation, just a whisper of a "sorry", she scurries off.

Si stands alone, riding a raft of emotions; then, anger, the rock in the rapids he finally hits. He hurls the gold pebbles at the river, releasing a thunderclap of hurt from within.

The river is left alone – but not for long. The boy known as Arlo, still in school armour, appears and, at this point, is quite ignorant of what the river is about to offer.

OUTRUNNING

PETER BARRON

When he was told he had Parkinson's Disease, Keith Wilson thought his running days were over. A keen amateur athlete, he'd always bought his running shoes well in advance, but they were given away – still in their boxes – as he tried to come to terms with the devastating diagnosis.

"I just thought that was it. I was facing life as a couch potato," he recalls.

But he couldn't have been more wrong. Two years on, seventy-one-year-old Keith is using running – as well as cycling, rock climbing and singing in a choir – as part of his strategy to hold back the disease. Just recently, he completed his mission to walk and run the distance from Land's End to John o'Groats. He started on New Year's Day 2022, and dedicated himself to running fifty miles a week. He finished in May 2022 with a walk along Hadrian's Wall.

Along the way, he's raised £650 for Parkinson's UK, and later topped that up to £1,000 by tackling the Lake District Ultra Challenge in June 2022, walking 100 kilometres over two days.

"There's no doubt that it's helping me to live with Parkinson's," says Keith, who resides in Middleton One Row, near Darlington. "It would have been easy to wallow in self-pity, but being active has helped me."

Keith was born in Murton, East Durham, where his dad worked on the coalface at the local pit. His own career was in education, lecturing in history and management at Darlington College and ending up as Director of Higher Education before going on to work part-time for Teesside and Sunderland Universities during retirement.

Keeping fit has always been part of his life, first with climbing, then playing squash. He took up running thirty-five years ago, becoming a keen member of the North York Moors Athletics Club. Keith participated in fell runs that included climbs up Roseberry Topping and to Captain

Cook's Monument. He's also a keen parkrunner, mainly in Darlington's South Park, alongside the River Skerne – with a personal best for the five-kilometre run clocked at 00:22:40.

When he was diagnosed with Parkinson's in March 2020, it came as something of a relief, because he had feared he might have a brain tumour. His legs had started turning to jelly, and he'd noticed his foot dragging on the floor. His voice had become slurred, and a tremor had developed in his hand.

"I knew something was wrong and, although it could have been worse, it still hit me hard," he says.

Keith hit a low ebb on his seventieth birthday when his climbing friends had arranged a Zoom call and he didn't want to take it. "That just wasn't me, and I realised I was very down."

The turning point came when he agreed to five weeks of intensive speech therapy, having initially rejected it. "Parkinson's destroys the link between the brain and the muscles, and I started to learn techniques to get them back in line. It gave me confidence. I stopped looking so frail, and I thought, if I can do it with my speech, maybe I can do it with my legs. It was a question of applying the same principles – mind over matter."

When he was sixty-eight – the year before his diagnosis – he'd bought a t-shirt with the slogan ALL MEN ARE BORN TO RUN BUT ONLY THE BEST ARE STILL RUNNING IN THEIR 70S. He'd hung it in his wardrobe, in readiness for his seventieth birthday, and it proved to be the inspiration to resume his active lifestyle.

"I spotted it one day, and I said to myself: 'It's time to get out there again,'" he says.

People with Parkinson's have low levels of dopamine, the neurotransmitter that produces adrenaline and acts as a chemical messenger, communicating signals between nerve cells in the brain and the rest of the body. Keith has seen how being active can generate dopamine, and therefore adrenaline, which helps him hold back the effects of Parkinson's.

"Exercise is recommended for all Parkinson's patients," he says, "and I would certainly endorse that, having seen the change in the way I feel since going back to being active.

"The adrenaline you get from going downhill on a bike, or climbing a rockface, makes you feel more normal. As for running, it comes from having targets. Every runner in the parkrun is a target to aim at, and if I don't have that to focus on, I lose everything. Now, if my legs turn to jelly, I tell myself it's a false message and crack on."

Laughing and singing also generate dopamine and adrenaline, so Keith has joined the Darlington SING Community Choir. He's turned into a musical runner, singing to himself while he completes his three laps of South Park on Saturday mornings. Through the choir, he met Darlington artist William E. Rees, and they enjoy long walks together, discussing art along the way and keeping Keith's mind active as well as his body.

Now fully retired with his wife, Jill Brannan, Keith is making the most of life with his two stepdaughters and deriving lots of happiness from nine-month-old granddaughter Phoebe.

With the Land's End-to-John o'Groats challenge behind him, he's focusing on the Lake District Ultra Challenge, determined to raise as much as he can for the charity that has supported him.

"Parkinson's UK helped me to come to terms with my diagnosis and gave me strategies to learn to live with it, so I want to give something back," he says. "I'm also happy to talk to anyone with Parkinson's – to give them a lift and explain that it's not the end of the road."

Keith knows there are plenty of challenges ahead – but it's great to see he's got Parkinson's Disease on the run.

TIPSTER

MARK JAMES CHAPPELL

A good tip, if ever you need to entertain a small child – say, when you become a father – is this: fold down the index finger of your left hand so that the top half, above the knuckle, cannot be seen; take the thumb of your right hand, similarly bend this in half and then use the tip of this hand's index finger to hide the knuckle. Now for the showstopper: fit the top half of the right-hand thumb on the bent-down left-hand index finger and slide up and down: to a small child, at the right angle, it looks as though you have a severed or detachable finger. Depending on the small child, they are either delighted or sickened.

It was my grandfather who taught me this, my mother's father; Norman, his name was, and he lived in a small village in County Durham. We would visit during school holidays, and it was there on the banks of the River Skerne that I first learned that no one in my family was at all interested in fishing.

Norman, though, would take me. A restless soul, he always seemed keen to get out of the house. He would tie a piece of string to a stick we found along the way, then tell me to drop it in the water. Bait, there was none. There was no point, as I was too young to be allowed a hook to put on it – and too stupid, it would seem, to realise that this greatly harmed my chances of reeling in a trout. I suppose I learned patience.

As I stood there in all weather for hours on end, unknowingly waiting for a miracle, Norman sat hunched in a fold-up chair, a folded-up newspaper in his lap and a small red pen held tightly in his hand. It wasn't until I was older that I realised that he, too, was waiting for a miracle.

The folded-up newspaper was *The Racing Post*. At the time, when I took a peek and saw pages upon pages of strange numbers and codes, incomprehensible to the layman, I assumed he was involved in government espionage at a high level. This was not case. No, he was studying the form.

He didn't live in this part of the world for the peace and quiet, or for the wonders of Nature, but for the race courses. His house was equidistant from Sedgefield, Catterick and Redcar. Too tall to be a jockey and too lazy to hold down a regular job, Norman scraped together a meagre existence as a tipster. Meagre, because his extensive network of local stable lads – history would seem to bear out – was spectacularly ill-informed.

What little he earned, he would reinvest. He was not a high roller, but preferred instead to bet small on improbable long shots and Byzantine trifectas that never came in; this, despite his golden rule never to back a horse he had tipped. It is only now, when I think back, that I wonder if such a capricious lifestyle had an influence on his character, which was often described as *volatile*; it is true that he was susceptible to violent mood swings.

His wife, Doris, my mother's mother, had a lot to put up with. She was not the archetypal 'sweet and gentle' grandmother, but mean-spirited and cantankerous, especially if she lost at cards – although this was rare, because of the ruthless manner in which she played, even against us children. "Newmarket" was her game of choice. Pocket money that had been carefully stockpiled for months prior to a visit would, come bedtime, disappear into her purse, and, as we children wept in the vain hope that the money would be returned, she would grumble to herself that *she* had been cheated.

But she was allowed. She had had a hard life, my mother insisted, a euphemism that chillingly conjured no end of terrible crimes; perhaps it was one such terrible crime that accounted for the missing tops of three of her fingers on her right hand, a detail that always held us in awe, even through tears, as she scooped her winnings off the card table.

Not yet a toddler, she had crawled to the bottom of her garden where her father was chopping wood. (At this point in the story, what happened to the those distal phalanges becomes all too apparent ...) Unaware of her approach, her father – my mother's grandfather, my great-grandfather – chopped and chopped. Doris reached up and put her hand on the bit of stump used for chopping wood, and down came the axe.

Her father was, of course, distraught, and, as a kind of penance, carried the three little fingertips in his pocket for months, wrapped in tissue inside a matchbox, until, finally – I think it was at Christmas – his father, my great-great-grandfather, wrested them from him and tossed them into an open fire. *There, now that's done,* he said, and life went on.

Unfortunately, I didn't hear this story until much later in life, long after both grandparents had died. And so, as I stood there on the banks of the River Skerne and watched as my grandfather performed the severed/detachable finger trick, I was naturally paralysed with fear; surely the evidence would suggest that my grandfather had practised on my grandmother first, and only perfected it after three failed attempts!

THE GREAT TOMATO TRAIN RESCUE

CHRIS LLOYD

When a tomato train slid off the East Coast Main Line and became bogged down in a County Durham carr, it took more than ten days for it to be freed – partly because the rescue operation was hampered, improbably, when a US jet fell out of the sky and crashed in a fireball into a field beside it. As well as the plane and train crashes, there was an unfortunate automobile accident and a runaway tractor incident. Perhaps most extraordinarily, no human was harmed – although one eyewitness reported that several wagonfuls of tomatoes were reduced to a red, porridgey mess.

At least the people of South Durham got to feast on free (intact) tomatoes.

The drama began in the early hours of Friday 7 May 1965, when the signalman controlling the East Coast Main Line at Preston-le-Skerne, to the east of Newton Aycliffe, put a slow goods train into a passing loop to allow the newspaper train behind it to speed past, north to Newcastle. The goods train was pulled by engine D350, and included in its cargo was a large quantity of tomatoes.

But the driver of D350 misread the signals. He failed to slow down so that the curve of the Preston loop would take him back onto the mainline. When he realised his error, he put the brakes on hard – but the weight of the train caused it to slide off the rails and into the bog.

This is the Isles area of South Durham, so named because the farmland here is perched on top of slightly raised ground, above boggy carrs. It was once a prehistoric lake, and little streams flow through the carrs into the Skerne. Railwaymen knew it as "the Ponderosa", because the watery land around the mainline wobbled when a fast train went through.

THE GREAT TOMATO TRAIN RESCUE

As D350 toppled, the wagons behind it jackknifed across the mainline. Minutes later, the newspaper train – the 1N02 from Manchester to Newcastle pulled by D352, another English Electric Type 4 diesel locomotive – smashed into them.

Railway workers reacted quickly to the accident. In the dark, despite the isolated location of the crash site, bundles of newspapers were carried across the fields to a fleet of lorries, which took them to Newcastle before dawn: the residents of the city would still awaken to find their morning newspapers waiting.

But little could be done for D350, even though a small army of railwaymen had marched over, armed with spades, to try and dig it out. The engine was slowly sinking into the bog, and could not easily be hauled out. They left it half buried in gravel and water until the necessary heavy haulage equipment could be assembled.

This allowed the railwaymen to turn their attention to the contents of the wagons.

"There were blokes there from all over South Durham," remembers Mike Hogg, from Strensall in York. "We trekked across the fields carrying picks and shovels and found eight or ten wagons on the floor which had sprayed the tomatoes everywhere.

"The gaffer said, 'Help yourselves to tomatoes.' I didn't, because although my mother was a great cook she was absolutely hopeless with sandwiches, and I knew all I would get was tomato sandwiches for weeks; but our gang vans were used as lorries to take the tomatoes round to people's houses."

Trevor Horner, of Bishop Auckland, was seventeen at the time, and tells a similar story. He was a junior technical assistant in the district engineer's office, and at the start of a lifelong railway career. "The site access was through the farms, and when we arrived, people were pushing rail bogies, or trolleys, loaded mounds-high with tomatoes," he says. "The loss adjustor had been and had written everything off so it was all scrap.

"My boss said, 'Get in that boxcar and get as many tomatoes as you can.' I had to perch on the side of this wagon and literally rolled my sleeves up and was pulling whole tomatoes out of this porridge of smashed tomatoes – I must have got twenty or thirty boxes out. They were taken back to the office and shared out.

"My share went to my aunt, who ran the VG shop at the top of Redworth Road in Shildon. She paid me trade price, so I got a bit of pocket money, and the tomatoes were washed off and sold."

(While South Durham was flooded with this glut of liberated tomatoes, such a shortage ensued in Newcastle that the price of tomatoes there shot up by 50 per cent.)

Back at the crash site, railwaymen covered the £100,000 locomotive with a tarpaulin and began preparations for the rescue. They dammed a stream and pumped out water to make the ground stable, and burrowed beneath the loco so steel hausers could be tied around it.

Five days after D350 had left the track, on Thursday 12 May, a £300,000 USAF Super Sabre jet crashed two fields away from where the railwaymen were at work. It was so near to them they could feel the blast.

The American pilot, Captain Marshall M. Kroot, had been flying to RAF Lakenheath in East Anglia when black smoke began billowing from his engine. He maydayed the newly civilian Teesside Airport at Middleton St George to try and land there, but then spotted the empty carrs beneath him and decided to ditch instead, pressing the 'eject' button as the plane plummeted.

Isaac Elders of Swan Carr Farm saw it coming so close to him that he threw himself out of his tractor in fright, causing the vehicle to run off into a hedge bottom. His wife, Muriel, saw the plane bounce across the field. "It was a terrifying sound, and there were bangs and cracks all over as bullets exploded," she told *The Northern Echo*. "Everything seemed to be going like a whirlwind. There was fire everywhere."

The explosion brought down power lines, cutting off the supply to the railway signals: once again, the East Coast Main Line ground to a halt.

Happily, Captain Kroot was practically unscathed. He was discovered nearby with his parachute, his ejector seat, a fully-inflated emergency dinghy, some maps and ration tins and a sore shoulder.

A US Air Force investigation team immediately flew from Lakenheath to Leeming to collect him. *The Northern Echo* reported: "During the journey from Leeming with a police car escort, their bus was involved in collision with another car and although no one was hurt, it delayed the start of the investigation."

Once the Americans had taken their plane away and power had been restored to the mainline, the railwaymen were able to set Sunday 23 May as the date to shut the mainline once more and extricate D350 from the carr. They brought two 75-ton cranes to the scene, one from Gateshead and the other from York, and began lifting at 4 AM. The hausers were wrapped around the stricken 133-ton loco, and the cranes pulled it upright. It was then detached from its bogies – the heavy wheels – and the Gateshead crane lifted the top half of the locomotive up. It was left dangling in midair while the York crane tried to lift the wheels from the mud. After nearly twelve hours, the bogies came free – with an "almighty squelch", according to *The Evening Despatch* – and the crane lifted them onto the track. The Gateshead crane lowered the top half back onto its wheels, and at 4 PM, D350 was pushed back gingerly to Darlington. It was scrubbed down and repaired, and the engine that had hauled the troubled tomato train worked for another twenty years.

THE HOMECOMING

MICHAEL DREW

What on Earth am I doing here? I ask myself, holding the remains of a father I never knew while thinking of another who was never really mine in the first place. In answer to my question, the river remains silent, slivers of pale October sunshine rippling across its slow, implacable surface as I feel a shiver run through me. The wind has always been cold down here by the Skerne, relentless, piercing gusts forever whipping along its banks as though driven by a will of their own. That never used to bother Dad, though. Come wind, rain or shine, he loved being down here, surrounded by the sights and sounds of Nature, listening for the murmur of moorhens in the bullrushes or the warbling of baby starlings in their nests. The next icy blast sends fallen autumn leaves rushing around my ankles in an ancient skitter of sound, while somewhere in the distance, hidden among the faraway trees, the joyous squeals of children compete with one another for my attention. For a moment I'm curious to know if they're the ones who left behind the muddy, yellow football I can see bobbing serenely among the reeds of the far bank.

How many other forgotten remnants must the Skerne have claimed over the years, I wonder; how many other lost toys and faded memories, carried away on its slow, ceaseless journey towards the sea? It's certainly seen its fair share of mine. But did they all reach the open ocean, in the end, set free to drift upon the tides wherever the current might take them? Or did some of them get caught up along the way, trapped in the shallows like this lonely little ball that reminds me so much of my childhood?

● ● ●

"You stop right there, Katie Green!" calls my dad across the intervening years, patiently rolling up his trouser legs and removing his shoes and socks. "I've told you before. You're not to step foot in this river without me or your mother's permission."

"But it's going to float away," I protest, torn between the anxiety of losing my brand-new frisbee and my father's ever-present irritation, referring to Sheila as my "mother" – a woman who, in truth, I can only remember as a warm, soft shadow, singing sweetly above my bed, but whose memory I still hold sacred.

"Don't be daft," chides my father, taking a step towards the river. "Do you really think I'd let that happen?"

No, I realise, of course I don't; he would walk to the ends of the Earth for me if I asked him to, and I know it. Looking back, that must have been one of the things that made Sheila so uneasy around me. In my girlish ignorance, I had always thought her cold and spiteful, chiefly because I wasn't *hers*; but now I can see just how threatened she must have been. It can't have been easy, fitting into such a complicated household, having to compete for her husband's love and attention with a girl as desperately determined to hang on to his affections as I was.

"Daaaaad, what are you doing?" calls Ange, her voice carried on the wind as she totters clumsily after us, my old Thomas the Tank Engine wellies still far too big for her, while the hand-me-down jacket she has on is at least two sizes too small. Behind her, in the distance, Sheila follows: a slow, silent figure outlined in black, set against a grey, tumultuous sky. She and Ange became distracted by a tangle of ripening blackberries on the way down here, but Dad hadn't seemed to notice, and I definitely wasn't going to say anything. I have come to cherish every moment Dad and I have alone; having time, just the two of us, is getting harder and harder now that Ange is older and eager enough to follow me wherever I go, to the point where, after six months, I feel like I have a second shadow.

"Are you blind or just stupid?" I call back at her, rolling my eyes. "He's getting my new frisbee out of the river ... obviously."

"Katie! Don't talk to your sister that way. It wasn't a stupid question at all."

THE HOMECOMING

"She's *not* my sister," I say, stamping my foot in frustration. "She's only my *half*-sister. It's not the same." But by the way Dad looks at me, I know I've gone too far. I wasn't trying to be mean – at least I don't think I was – but sometimes I just wish Ange and Sheila would stay at home for a change.

"Do you want me to get this frisbee for you or not?" snaps Dad, all his usual warmth and kindness suddenly absent.

"Yes, please," I reply, eyes on the ground, my words barely audible, even to myself. My father is not a man easily angered; but once stirred, his tempers can last for days if not handled with care.

"Then apologise to your sister. You are *both* my daughters, which means that she *is* your sister. Do you understand?"

"But Dad," I plead, in one last effort to make my point.

He's not having any of it. "That's enough, Katie! I won't ask you again."

"Okay, fine," I huff, looking away across a field scattered with the last few flowers of the year. "Ange, I'm so –"

"Mum says that Dad's not your real dad either," interrupts Ange, her brow knitted in defiance, upper lip pushed out into a petulant little pout that I shall never forget. "She says you're a Drop-Dead. I'm not supposed to tell you because it's a secret, but she says everyone knows."

It takes me a moment to process what she is trying to say, but despite her confusion, Ange's eyes remain clear and unashamed as she speaks. She is neither smart nor sly enough to make up something so poisonous on her own, so of course she must be mistaken. She must have misheard something somewhere, or gotten her lines crossed. I'm not adopted.

But as I turn to my father, waiting for him to put right this ridiculous notion, I feel my stomach give a sudden lurch as if I've just been thrown out of an airplane, or dropped off the side of Blackpool Tower. His eyes are no longer stern with anger, but wide with alarm, his huge, mountainous chest contracting with a sharp intake of breath which is quickly cut short by the whirling shriek of a snipe, bursting from the reeds nearby, disturbed it seems, by my now-long-forgotten frisbee.

* * *

A Drop-Dead ... not your real dad ... Ange's words echo in my ears as I look down at the small, ceramic urn clutched between my frozen fingers. It took me a long time to find my 'real dad' in the end, but after years of searching, I discovered that he wasn't really cut out for the job. I shouldn't have been surprised, I suppose; after all, he did run out on me the day I was born, leaving me both fatherless *and* motherless within my first few hours of life.

His betrayal felt no less cowardly when he tried to explain it to me thirty years later, crammed into the corner of a hot, stuffy café in the Midlands, a pair of untouched mugs of tea sat cooling on the tabletop between us. I was surprised by his choice of venue, but what really struck me most about him as he talked was how much *older* he was than I had ever imagined him, how small and frail he seemed, that rough, intermittent cough interrupting every other word as he tried to justify his decision that day, those gnarled, tobacco-stained fingers gripping the table as if it were a life raft and he, a sailor lost at sea.

I found that I was not ready to hear his reasons for that day or any other, before that horrible, rasping cough caught up with him. Maybe that's why he left this final task to me. Maybe he hoped to gain my forgiveness by allowing me this last act of absolution; then again, maybe he just had no one else left to do it. His Last Will and Testament held no more clues to his life story than his, short, clipped efforts at small talk the day we met, but for some reason I found that I could not deny him his last request. Not because I owed it to him, I try to tell myself, but because *he* owed it to *me*. The truth, however, is that this morning's last-minute decision to go to his funeral was as unexpected as Ange's revelation here on the riverbank.

Staring down into the cold, silent depths of the river gliding by, the question returns: *What am I doing here?* The remains of the man inside this urn have about as much connection to this place as he did to me while he was alive. But still, this is where I find myself, no closer to understanding *why* than I was when I pulled off the drive this morning, hot, slick tears blurring the road in front of me as I switched my mobile phone to silent. Jeremy would only have started to worry if he'd known where I was going. Nevertheless, I still managed to miss the funeral, just as I had with Dad's and Sheila's; that, however, is where the similarities end.

I had not been hurrying along the M40, weaving through traffic and speeding to beat red lights as Dad's and Sheila's memorial service had begun. No, I had been sobbing hopelessly on the couch at home as Jeremy tried desperately to get the live video link up and running – an obstacle made necessary by the same worldwide catastrophe that had taken both my parents within a week of each other. By the time we managed to fix the problem, the few, socially distanced family members able to attend were already singing the last hymn of the service. A pair of heavy, blue curtains blocked the caskets from sight as I looked on, heartbroken, restricted to an over-the-shoulder view of a priest I had never met, in a church I did not recognise.

I thought I had had a good understanding of loss before they died, but now I know I hadn't even scratched the surface. Luckily, Jeremy was there to help me through it. I don't know what I would have done without him cooking my meals and giving me a reason to get out of bed in the morning. I wish Dad had gotten to meet him before he died. Things between us were never quite the same after Ange let slip his little secret. For years, he tried to console me, but as time went on, his protestations and assurances of love only seemed to make things worse. Deep down, I knew that he loved me, and that he always would; but for some reason, I could never bring myself to believe that he could love me as much as he loved Ange, or Sheila, or even as much as the poor barren woman whose idea it had been to adopt me in the first place. For their part, Sheila and Ange always tried to make up for their mistake: Ange, perpetually doe-eyed and needy in her apologies; Sheila, always meek and sincere in hers. The two of them ended up tiptoeing around me for years afterwards, cowed, I think, by the overwhelming sense of loss and desolation that hung over me back then.

Inevitably, though, it was I who abandoned them rather than the other way around, running off down south to start a new life as soon as I left school. For years I spent my days washing bedsheets and my evenings serving drinks, surviving on as little as five hours of sleep a night, doing anything and everything necessary to make it on my own. We all kept up appearances after I left, of course, and we even managed some happy times together over the years – probably more than I ever gave us credit for. But I still felt the need to maintain that geographical distance, that physical buffer against the kind of pain and suffering that I knew loving people too deeply could lead to.

It was the same in my personal life until I met Jeremy, with his quietly romantic gestures and patient but persistent efforts to get me to meet him after work. Before then, however, it was as if not knowing where I came from had cut me adrift from the rest of the world, instilling in me the need to write my own backstory as well as forge my own future in isolation. The day Dad died, I finally came to realise what becoming unmoored from society really felt like. At the bottom of the void he left behind was a place where highs and lows no longer mattered, where everything I cared about was suddenly consumed by numb sterility.

Jeremy has done his best to keep my head above water since the funeral, but after everything else that has happened, there's not much more I think he can do for me. I'm the only one who can dispel this dark cloud that has laid claim to my life these past six months. So maybe that's why I'm here, shivering in the fading light of autumn, freezing my toes off by this old, winding river, wondering if this is where my backstory is to be found, or if, in fact, this is where it should end.

As I try to focus, the scenery around me seems to swell and reverberate with so many memories that its reality starts to elude me, past and present merging like the rumble of traffic on the motorway nearby, each driver on their own journey, for their own reasons, but all ultimately still bound for the same destination. Apart from the road, the rest of the world seems to have fallen asleep around me. The kids have all gone home, and the few rabbits that were here are holed up in their burrows. I am alone. Even the setting sun has now disappeared behind the clouds skirting the horizon. I close my eyes and listen for a sign as to what I should do, but everything around me – even the cold, immutable presence of the urn in my hands – suddenly feels so transient and insubstantial that I have to open my eyes again just to make sure that I'm still here.

Looking down at the small, grey pot no larger than that cold cup of tea in the Midlands, I feel the same sense of dislocation I have felt for most of my adult life, unsure as to whether or not I can ever truly know myself if I can't even bear to sit down, face-to-face, with where I really come from.

I may never know myself, but at least I know this place, and it still knows me. It's probably seen more sides to me than any of the various mothers and fathers I've lost over the years, more than any friend or enemy I've made. It knew me in the days before Dad met Sheila, and in the long, confusing years afterwards. It knew me in the moments before my first kiss, and has borne witness to every fight and cigarette I've ever had. It's seen the happiest moments of my life, and been replenished by my bitterest tears. It knows me in the way Dad always tried know me, even after I abandoned him in search of the cold, grey ashes in front of me.

What about Ange? I wonder, almost absentmindedly. Did she ever come to understand herself in a way that I could not? Did the firm foundations of her childhood help her to cope when our parents died? Or does she still struggle to make sense of what happened?

I should have asked her, I reflect sorrowfully, taking a step towards the river, the stiff, dry scrape of the urn running through me like a ghost walking over my grave as I unscrew its lid, the sound as jarring and incongruous as a full stop in the middle of a sentence.

Then, from somewhere far away, I hear a voice, far deeper and more worn-out than I remember, but still unmistakably *hers*.

"Katie, is that you?" calls Ange, her thin, weary face flushed from the cold, loose white hair poking out from beneath a woollen hat that I recognise as one of Sheila's.

Turning to meet her eyes, I hear the wind blow a long, sombre note from the depths of the urn as wisps of fine, grey dust evaporate into the air around us, subsumed by this landscape that never seems to change, yet never stops moving.

"My God, Katie, I *thought* it was you," Ange says, her astonished smile tinged with a hint of concern. "What on Earth are you doing here?"

PLANE SAILING: THE FLIGHT OF THE *STORMBIRD*

PETER BARRON

Like two streams flowing inexorably toward a river, a pair of admirable initiatives in Darlington just had to come together sooner or later. The first is Discover Brightwater, a £3.3 million landscape partnership dedicated to celebrating life around the Skerne (of which this very volume is part). The second, Plane Sailing for Heroes, is a community-interest company devoted to supporting military veterans through woodwork projects, the flagship of which is the building of a replica of a Viking longboat – provisionally named *Stormbird.*

As someone who has written about both Discover Brightwater and Plane Sailing for

Heroes, it struck me that they really ought to be in the same boat, as it were. An introduction was duly made, which led to the launch of a formal partnership between the two organisations.

For its part, Discover Brightwater, which is supported by the National Lottery Heritage Fund, has pledged £5,000, as well as support in financing training workshops. In return, Plane Sailing for Heroes has agreed that the River Skerne will be the entirely appropriate setting for the longboat's maiden voyage, by which time she may well sail under the name of *Brightwater Stormbird*.

"It's the perfect fit, a match made in Heaven," says Bob Marshall, the affable driving force behind Plane Sailing for Heroes. "This partnership with Discover Brightwater gives us an anchor that connects what we are doing with the area we are invested in."

The romantic idea to build a Viking longboat began a few years ago at the Phoenix House Recovery Centre at Catterick Garrison, where Bob was working for Help for Heroes as part of the mental health and wellbeing team. As a woodshop manager, he used his lifelong passion for carpentry to support the recovery of those who'd suffered physical or mental trauma in war zones. He wanted the veterans to have the chance to work on something ambitious, and had the unlikely idea of building a Viking longship.

Discussions with the Viking Ship Museum in the Danish city of Roskilde led to the receipt of plans for a thirty-foot-long vessel, called a Skuldelev (named after the Danish waterway in which five eleventh-century ships were found), and construction started in the summer of 2019 with up to 120 veterans involved in the project. Sadly, the schedule was scuppered by Covid-19, which led to the closure of Phoenix House; but Bob was determined to carry on supporting veterans.

Along with boat-builder Mike Holtham, he launched Plane Sailing for Heroes. The frame of *Stormbird* left Phoenix House in December 2021, and was transported to Darlington to be stored at a workshop leased by Darlington Timber Supplies.

The move to Darlington also led to a rethink of the design for the boat's figurehead. Instead of the phoenix that was originally planned, it will now be based on the wyvern that appears on the town's coat of arms.

Meanwhile, a dedicated group of volunteers readied the workshop, bringing in around £60,000 worth of their own equipment and installing an accessible toilet, breakout facilities and a dust extractor before the first veterans arrived to begin their training to work on the Viking longboat. The £5,000 grant from Discover Brightwater is likely to be spent on other vital health-and-safety additions to the equipment onsite.

With a fair wind, the longboat should be shipshape for a launch somewhere on the Skerne sometime in 2024.

"It's just brilliant to have this kind of support – it feels like it was meant to be," says Bob.

Discover Brightwater programme manager Paul Black is equally as enthusiastic about the potential for the partnership. "Our remit is to 'reveal, restore and celebrate life on and around the Skerne' and, when we heard about the project to provide therapeutic training for military veterans by building a Viking longship, it had our name written all over it," he says, smiling. "The preservation and revival of ancient heritage skills is a very important theme for us, so we have worked closely with Plane Sailing to provide training workshops this past year. And, naturally, we're really keen to work with our partners to explore how the maiden voyage can take place on the Skerne itself, or a watercourse linked to the river."

With new partners pulling in the same direction and latter-day warriors setting a new course for their skills and energies, the voyage of the *Brightwater Stormbird* is already well underway. All that remains is for the river to carry it to completion.

OUR HOUSE

FRAN EDWARDS

"What are you doing in my house!"

We froze, my sister like a statue, with her hand still on the window she had just been peering through. Technically it was a false accusation, as we were in his garden and not in his house – but the look on his face, and the fact that he was pointing an air rifle at us, made that seem irrelevant.

"You bastards from the Council never give up, do you! Sneaking round when you think I'm out!"

I found my voice first. "No, no, you're mistaken; we're not from the Council, we're just –"

"Now you're lying as well as trespassing!" He spat the words at us, waving the air rifle around in an alarming way. "'Course you're from the Council. Look at you, in your smart suits, thinking you're better than everyone else."

"Well, actually, we've been to a funeral."

My sister's words seemed to confuse him; he lowered the rifle. With the removal of that threat, I could focus on his face. He was unshaven, with grey, unkempt hair, and his shirt was a bit grubby: a man who looked like he didn't bother much about his personal appearance. His anger had given him a vigour that belied his years. Now his voice was quieter, but still hostile.

"That doesn't explain why you were snooping, looking in my windows. This is *my house*!"

"And it was ours, a long time ago," my sister said quietly. "We were both born in this house."

● ● ●

Twenty minutes later, we were sitting in his kitchen while he pottered about boiling the kettle, warming the teapot and finding some slightly stale biscuits. His name was Bill, and he'd lived there since he'd got married in 1977. "Forty-five years," he told us proudly, "though

I've been alone for the last five. Sadly, we couldn't have children, but we built a good life together."

We told him how the death of our Auntie had brought us here together for the funeral, and we'd come a day earlier to explore old haunts. We'd seen the building where our father had worked, which used to be the town hall. We'd enjoyed tea and scones in the department-store café, where he would come to meet us and our mother after he finished on a Saturday at lunchtime. We'd walked up Sugar Hill to see the primary school we'd both attended, though I was only there for six weeks before we moved. The thing we hadn't managed to fit in to our nostalgic itinerary till then was a visit to our old house.

Inspired by our words, Bill began reminiscing about the street "back in the day", stirring our memories till we were prompting each other's stories.

The patch of rough land at the end of the road where a bonfire was built each 5th November, where everyone would gather to share food and watch the fireworks display. The little wood opposite which was an adventure playground for us children, in the days when everything seemed more free and easy.

"Weren't the summers always sunny back then?"

The picnics we had in South Park on sunny Sundays. That old tartan blanket our dad used to spread out on the grass, close to where the willows dipped their trailing branches into the lazy water of the Skerne.

Bill smiled and reached for another biscuit. "Do you remember the Ketteridge family – the one with all those kids, and a mother who couldn't control them?" We certainly did; my sister recalled scrapping in the middle of the street with one of them because he'd been mean to me. "Mrs Ketteridge is ninety-one now, quite eccentric. Wears fluorescent pink wellies whatever the time of year or weather." He chuckled. "But she's been a good neighbour, would never see you go wanting for anything she could lend or give you.

"My wife Emily loved this house. This is where I'm going to end my days, and no heartless officials with their 'Compulsory Purchase Order' are going to stop me." The passion in his voice made me glance at the air rifle now propped casually against the cupboard door. I felt an anxiety that had nothing to do with my own safety.

When it was time to go, we stood up and thanked Bill for his hospitality.

"Being able to come inside our house has been the most important part of the trip," I told him as I took his hand. He placed his other hand on top of mine and gave a gentle squeeze.

"My guess is you were both born in the double bedroom upstairs," he said. "Would you like to take a look?"

* * *

In the taxi back to the train station, we shared our pleasure and appreciation of that act of kindness and shook our heads in disbelief at how the events of the afternoon had unfolded. We had wished Bill well, trying to be encouraging – but remaining cautious in our encouragement. His mind, however was made up; this meant too much to him, and there was no room for compromise. When we left, I had given him my mobile number – more as a gesture of goodwill than with any real expectation that he would use it.

Life fell back into its usual routine, and apart from getting out the family photo album one evening and indulging in a bit more nostalgia, I hadn't really thought much about Bill.

About a month after our visit, I had a phone call from my sister. She launched straight in with: "Have you seen the news! It's Bill – his one-man stand against the Council. The press are making a big thing of it."

I logged onto a newsfeed, and there he was: Bill, outside the house, defiant as ever, with homemade placards pleading his case and denouncing the Council. (Fortunately, the air rifle was nowhere in sight.) There were plans to bring in the bulldozers over the next couple of days to finish the demolition, which would clear all the houses from this piece of land. A portly councillor explained to a reporter that the Council would be putting this land to "good use", and that the current occupant had been offered generous, highly suitable alternative accommodation, which for some reason he kept refusing. The councillor cited another resident, a lady in her nineties, who had accepted their offer and was delighted with her new accommodation. An image flashed through my mind of Mrs Ketteridge, walking away from her past in her pink wellies. I hoped she wouldn't be watching now, as the camera scanned the flattened land where her home had stood for so many years.

"We should do something," I said.

"But what can we do?" my sister asked.

She had a point, and I had no answer. "I'll think about it," was all I could find by way of reply.

● ● ●

After breakfast the next day, I was clearing the pots away when I received a text on my phone. I assumed it would be my husband, who'd gone to the shops but had left the shopping list on the kitchen table.

But it was Bill. The text said simply, WISH ME LUCK, and there was a photo attached of him holding up a heavy chain with a large padlock and standing next to a placard that read: **THE SKERNE AVENUE ONE. THIS IS MY HOUSE.**

● ● ●

It being such short notice, we had to pay full price for the train tickets, but we both agreed that we had no choice. There was a circus of press, councillors, bystanders, local residents and men with hardhats, high-vis jackets and large, intimidating demolition equipment. I'm still not sure how we made it through to Bill; I guess we just used the confusion to our advantage. I remember wondering how my family would react, and feeling a little bit guilty that I had been less than honest with my husband. Still, he wouldn't be in ignorance for long. He never misses the six o'clock news, and tonight would be no exception.

Tonight, he would see footage of his wife, his sister-in-law and a man he'd never met, padlocked to the drainpipes of a house, holding up placards that read **THE SKERNE AVENUE ONE. THIS IS OUR HOUSE.** and shouting as loudly as they possibly could, to make sure their voices were heard:

"What are you doing in our house!"

NOBLE BEHEMOTHS OF THE SKERNE: SOUTH DURHAM'S CATTLE CHRONICLES

CHRIS LLOYD

Cattle with short horns have been bred along the east coast of Britain since Danish farmers first brought them over in the aftermath of the Viking raids, but the Brightwater area of South Durham is famed for developing a breed renowned for producing large quantities of milk and beef: the shorthorn, which celebrated its 200th anniversary in 2022.

In the eighteenth century, new techniques and a growth in the science of agriculture enabled pioneering farmers to breed larger, more productive animals. These advances were fuelled by urbanisation and turnipisation. As towns and cities grew during the Industrial Revolution, the countryside had to produce more food; assistance arrived in the form of the turnip, from Holland, in the 1730s. Cattle had traditionally been slaughtered on Martinmas (11 November) because of a lack of winter feed, but turnips allowed farmers to overwinter them. And so, munching on turnips, the cattle carried on growing.

This encouraged farmers to consider the genetic fitness of their animals, so that they grew bigger and faster and produced as much beef and milk, and tallow for candles, as possible. To this end, Michael Dobinson of The Isles – farmland raised above the boggy carrs between Newton Aycliffe and Sedgefield – went to Holland in the early eighteenth century and bought some bulls, adding a new dimension to the cattle of the Tees Valley; the resultant breed became known as "Teeswaters" or just "Durhams".

The first star of this new agricultural age was the Blackwell Ox, bred by Christopher Hill on his farm to the south of Darlington. Because of the ox's enormousness, it was the first to have its picture painted and distributed in the manner that a pop star hands out signed photos to fans. When it was slaughtered in Darlington in 1779, it weighed 151 stone 10 lbs (935 kg), and its beef was sold for a shilling a pound to the local leading families.

Many local farmers were experimenting with their breeding programmes, but the Colling brothers, Robert and Charles, of Ketton to the north of Darlington, were outstanding in their field. In 1784, Charles bought some extremely tasty veal on Darlington market and discovered that the father of the veal calves was an impressive-looking bull called "Hubback", which had been bred by John Hunter of Hurworth in 1777. Charles liked the veal so much, he bought the bull for 10 guineas. His wife Mary then spotted a fine cow in a field near Eryholme and persuaded the reluctant farmer, a Mr Maynard, to sell it and its calf. Thus two new additions, named "Lady Maynard" and "Young Strawberry", joined the Collings' herd. Then, at Darlington market, for £13, Charles bought a black and white cow bred on the Duke of Northumberland's Stanwick estate and named it "Duchess".

He now owned the four finest shorthorns in the district. From them, he bred Favourite, the great-grandson of Hubback, which sired three of the most internationally famous animals of the day. The first was the Ketton Ox, born in March 1796. When first exhibited at Darlington market in 1799, it weighed a whopping 216 stone (1,372 kg) and caused a sensation. In 1801, it was sold to showman farmer John Day of Lincolnshire, for £250. He renamed it the "Durham Ox" and built a special carriage for it. Pulled by four or six horses, it toured the country as a travelling curiosity. It didn't have an act as such – it didn't sing or tell jokes – but it did have its gargantuan girth, which people were prepared to pay to see.

The Durham Ox spent most of 1802 starring in London, where takings were £97 a day, equivalent to roughly over £6,000 today – a serious sum for the time. In the early winter of 1803, the Ox had a homecoming in South Durham: Darlington for one night only, followed by a quick stop in Ketton and a further break in Ferryhill before a twelve-night extravaganza in Newcastle. By the time it arrived in Hereford in 1806, it had covered 3,000 miles in five years. *The Northampton Mercury* billed it as "the greatest wonder of the age" and "the greatest curiosity in Europe": "In short, no language can give an adequate idea of the beauty, symmetry, and size of this extraordinary animal," said the newspaper. Admissions to see it at the Green Dragon Inn was one shilling for ladies and gentlemen, and 6d for servants and children.

The Durham Ox wasn't the biggest beast of its day, but Mr Day had created the best buzz. It was a good-looking, well-natured creature – "my wife who rode with him in the carriage found him harmless as a fawn and familiar as a lapdog," wrote Mr Day in his memoirs – and was surprisingly agile for so large an ox. Merchandise, such as prints, china plates and scale models, were produced as Mr Day milked his ox, and many of the communities they visited were so impressed that they named a pub after the bovine star. From Coundon to Warwick, you can still sip a pint in The Durham Ox. In the goldfields of Victoria, Australia, there is a hamlet called Durham Ox that is centred around a pub of the same name, opened in 1848 by prospectors from Derbyshire who were big fans of the ox from the Ketton outback.

The end for the Durham Ox began on 19 February 1807, when it arrived for a gig in Oxford. As it manoeuvred its bulk out of its carriage, it slipped, dislocating a hip. After eight weeks, it showed no sign of recovery. It was in pain; and Mr Day, to his credit, called in the butchers – three of them – to slaughter it. Despite having lost weight during its last two months after its accident, the monster weighed 271 stone (1,724 kg) when it died.

The next supersized superstar produced in Ketton was the Durham Ox's half-sister, the White Heifer. Born in 1896, it weighed 164 stone (1,043 kg) at the age of four, and Robert Colling sold it to The Three Kings Hotel in Piccadilly, London, where it was exhibited as "the greatest wonder in the world of the kind". Because it had journeyed from Ketton on the banks of the Skerne to the capital on the banks of the

Thames, it was known as "the White Heifer that travelled". It lived until at least 1811, when an artist painted it standing in front of a man slicing delicious-looking turnips. This image is on the pub bearing its name that opened in West Park, Darlington, in 2006.

Such was the Colling brothers' fame that King George III leased one of their bulls for three years to improve his herd in Windsor. But their biggest success was Comet, born in 1804: "He had a fine masculine head, broad and deep chest, shoulders well laid back, crops and loins good, hind quarters, long, straight and well-packed, thighs thick, breast full and well let-down, with nice straight hocks and hind legs," enthused Charles Colling. "He had fair sized horns, ears straight and hairy, and a grandeur of style and carriage that baffled description."

Because of the Collings' inbreeding programme, Comet's father and grandfather were the same bull, Favourite, who had been mated with its mother and its own daughter born by its own mother. A cow called "Phoenix" was, therefore, both of Comet's grandmothers.

Comet was the star of the sale when Charles, sixty, retired from farming. It became the first bull to sell for more than 1,000 guineas, making it the shorthorn equivalent of Trevor Francis, the first £1 million footballer – although Sir Henry Vane-Tempest, of Wynyard, rode up minutes after the hammer had come down and offered £1,600 cash to the syndicate that had bought Comet. They refused.

That day, Charles made £7,115 and 17 shillings by selling his forty-seven animals. "Well, we've beaten all England in prices and have no shorthorns left," his wife Mary said, sadly. They retired to Monkend Hall in Croft-on-Tees, where the pub on the opposite bank of the river is still called The Comet.

The syndicate, which included Colonel Trotter and Messrs Wetherall, Wright and Charge, kept Comet at Cleasby, a village on the outskirts of Darlington, for stud. Comet died in 1815 and was buried in a field – Comet's Garth – with a chestnut tree planted over it.

On 3 February 1865, the tree was chopped down, and Comet was disinterred. A 2-foot

1-inch rib was sent to California for Americans to marvel at the burger-making-potential of such a monster – but most of its ginormous remains ended up in a Darlington museum.

Charles's brother Robert continued farming at Barmpton, near Ketton, until his death in 1820. He was nicknamed "the Prince of the Skerne" and would, in fact, have been famed for his work breeding sheep if his cattle hadn't been so big. In his last years, in two sales – with prices affected by post-Napoleonic Wars depression – he sold 105 animals for more than £10,000.

And so the development of the shorthorn passed to a new generation. In the Brightwater area, they include Thomas Bates of Aydon Castle, near Corbridge, who was the first person to pay the Collings 100 guineas for a cow and who specialised in the dairy side of shorthorns – he sold butter at Newcastle market. He was left a legacy by his wonderfully named Aunt Joyous, which enabled him to buy a farm at Kirklevington, near Yarm, for £30,000 in 1811. (He paid £20,000 in cash.) He spent twenty years improving the ground until, in 1830, he deemed it ready, and moved his fifty shorthorns down from Northumbria.

In 1839, he put his favourites on a steamer from Middlesbrough and sailed them down to London. From there, they travelled by canal to Aylesbury to attend the first Royal Show in Oxford. Bates won First Prize.

Thomas Booth and his sons John and Richard farmed at Killerby, near Catterick, and Warlaby, near Ainderby Steeple. They developed the beef side of the shorthorns, and won First Prize at the second Royal Show, held in Cambridge.

These early animals changed the global face of farming. The first "Durhams" were exported to Virginia in the US in 1783, where it was discovered that their placid temperament made them ideal for pulling the wagons that set out for the West.

In 1812, Sir Henry Vane-Tempest shipped the Collings' Teeswaters to his estate in County Galway in Ireland, and in 1823 a shorthorn bull named Tarquin was exported from Teesdale to Buenos Aires. Tarquino, as it became known, is still regarded as the father of the Argentinian beef industry.

In 1812, the Colling brothers and Bates and Booth were present at a meeting at Sir Henry's home, Wynyard Hall, when the shorthorn breeders agreed that their pedigree records should be kept. They passed all their details to Gordon Coates of Pontefract, who began to compile them into a gigantic family tree, which he eventually published as *The Shorthorn Herd Book* in 1822. It was the first time anywhere in the world that such a feat had been attempted for cattle; thoroughbred horses had had their bloodlines chronicled since 1791.

In the summer of 2022, 200 shorthorns were taken to the Great Yorkshire Show to parade before their society's patron, Princess Anne, as a commemoration of the bicentenary of the breed, which began on the banks of Brightwater.

WHEREVER WENT THE RIVER

JOHN RIDSDALE

Nearly fifty years have passed since I first walked along this path, idly following a grassy bank that wound wherever the river went, the land made greener, *greater*, I'd say, by its never-ending, always-unfolding wend. I wasn't alone then, and I'm not alone now – though that's only true in essence, for the young girl who walked with me on that late summer day can no longer hold my hand. But memory has its imprint in primordial things, as if the itch I feel on my palm was where the damselfly landed but was never caught.

* * *

Her name was Jenny, and we were both nineteen in 1972. I suppose, in retrospect, our childhood was our courtship. We'd lived in the village our whole lives, neighbours and schoolfriends, playmates and companions, before sensing that the natural togetherness of our lives meant something deeper in our veins: a kind of blood-bond, a love that existed before we knew just how much meaning was attached to those feelings by our senses.

It wasn't gradual, and it wasn't unrealistic. It was *innate*. As I watched her grow up, I became aware of a strong disturbance in my equilibrium that, I soon realised, comprised the grit-like random epiphanies of sex. I could watch her walking down the street from a window, lose myself in the way she looked and then find myself wondering where I'd gone when I came back to my senses: a wonderful, wakeful unconsciousness. For a while I preferred to keep it secretive, as if telling her how I felt would destroy the fabulous joy of just watching her. But there came a time when the secret exploded naturally into words, and telling her how I felt was an act of faith: what I expected in return was also what she expected to give. *Sealed with a kiss.*

Although we were only teenagers, we were already uniquely bonded to our emotions – and emotions, at that age, are more important than the dull commodities of sunlight and air. The years passed; we grew up – but we didn't grow away. After leaving school our paths split, but there remained the old anchoring presence of our place and time in the world, and we adjusted to that world's turns with the surly equanimity of youth, which mainly entailed entrusting ourselves to complete ignorance of everything around us when we were back together.

I had an apprenticeship with a firm on the industrial estate, while she worked in a unisex boutique in town called "Garbage". I'd finish work and then take the long walk round to meet her, waiting for closing time when she'd drive us home in the battered tan Mini Cooper she'd acquired on her seventeenth birthday. Often, while waiting, I'd peer through the shop window, the gaudy display, like I was parting jungle leaves and trying not to startle parakeets.

Once I grew restless waiting and went inside, hanging around near the back among some racks of velveteen flares with embroidered hems while she served customers. She couldn't see me as I watched her, and when she stepped out from behind the counter I saw in a frighteningly precise moment just how frank her beauty was. She looked a picture. I took a mental Polaroid of this honey-eyed blonde unveiling a face as impassive as a nun's under harsh fluorescence shimmering towards aura, her body poured through a tangerine mini-dress loosely bolted at the waist by a silver chain belt that charmed her leanness down legs both long and fine, an asymmetric smile commanding diffidence, the slightest curve of her nose lending haughtiness to elegance. Perhaps this was the first time her beauty had hit me with such force. I found it phenomenal, as though the universe had unfolded itself before me with its smallest power and I'd observed a flower at its core. In some obscure way, it felt almost holy.

* * *

It may be natural to assume that, with such a love, and at such an age, I would be an utter slave to my desires, eager to prove my manhood by making love with her. That is only partially true: in fact, I was terrified. Abiding by the conventions of the age or disregarding them with abandon: this was a senseless battle for my conscience more than my psyche. Then, the biggest fear for any girl was an unwanted pregnancy; the biggest fear for any boy, a pregnant girlfriend. We weren't stupid, and despite wanting to be seen, somehow, to be as *modern* as our contemporaries when it came to sex, not adhering to those hidebound moral codes of premarital tolerances, the very idea of holding out was always close to anathema. So when we kissed and petted, we did so in the heaviest terms, stopped at the fragile gate of full sex only by those natural fears. In the end I let Jenny decide, and she decided on the pill, freeing me from responsibility – something for which I felt equally grateful and guilty.

Sex is strange – like a soft and tough battle fought out by two sides, in which winning and surrendering are each justification for the always-equitable end, where strength of love lies in its compassion. As we lay satisfied, I was blissfully sad there was only a lifetime to experience such joy when I wanted eternity. She would often call me "greedy" afterwards, as if the goodness of a thing could be rationed; but she always smiled when she said it.

The problem was not finding the time to make love, but finding the place. We rarely had either of our families' houses to ourselves, so we began taking long evening walks over fields that followed the course of the old river that threaded itself through the village. Here we found many bankside gullies and bushes with flat, grassy undergrowth, cool as a sheet, that we could use as our temporary beds. This was the River Skerne, and sometimes we stayed long into the next morning just watching the moonlight trying lazily to enlighten the water. I realised that some words are tokens of Antiquity. The moon was the coiner of this stretch of river, trying to stamp its presence onto something too molten to hold a royal image and leaving, instead, its delightful mirror. I became fascinated by the name, imagining its harsh tone formed like water through stone, and dripping first from Viking lips.

That summer, on our holidays, we'd often walk the slow miles beside the river in a trance of happiness, fretless over time and wayward with caring. I wondered if we could ever follow it back to its source, how long that would take, and what we might see on the way. Of the two of us, I'd always had more romantic notions, and when I whispered my thoughts to Jenny, she instantly became the great demolisher of dream.

"It leads to the sea," she said flatly.

But even the plain brutality of fact didn't deter me. I resolved that before our holidays were over, we'd follow it the other way, towards its end if not its beginning. And after some delay while heavy rain dampened my dream, the day arrived almost by instinct, unplanned, arrested by the weightless sense of *rightness* as I walked over to her house, the new sun's haze almost like a ceramic glaze in places against the walls, upon the rooftops, the shadows denser than meaning, and every window rippling like it was stained glass.

* * *

Jenny was in the kitchen, wrapping sandwiches in greaseproof paper and stowing them into a calico bag.

"Going somewhere?" I asked.

"*We* are," she said, a wry little smirk accenting her smile as she pulled two bottles of cider from the pantry. Along with a small transistor radio and her purse, these followed the sarnies into the bag. It was uncanny how well she could read and gauge my emotions without me even being there. Hale with anticipation, I was eager to set off, but Jenny dawdled while choosing a dress. Finally settling on a long, floral boho skirt and a floppy hat, she fluttered what-do-you-think eyes at me through her bedroom mirror.

"A bit long for walking through fields in," I suggested.

She tilted her head. "You're right," she sighed, before dashing to the kitchen to fetch a pair of scissors and proceeding to savage the hem till it was transformed into something ragged, a foot above knee-length. I trimmed a few threads off at the back and admired her legs, resisting the urge to stroke.

"Are we ready now?" I asked.

"Perfectly," she pouted, looking down on me, coquettish and prim at once as she pulled the back of the skirt in against her rump, censoring my glance.

Her parents at work, we had the place to ourselves – but the subtle resistance to lingering any longer near the bedroom was made more powerful by the urge to get going. It was nearly noon. We ran downstairs, grabbed the bag and, without another word, opened the door onto the idling day. From the slightly elevated back garden, the vista over Brafferton and Coatham Mundeville appeared as green and generous as Eden. I looked at Jenny and she looked at me, our skins bronzed by the long sun's benison. Then we stepped through the gate.

* * *

There is nothing as calming as walking without haste, and although we were not aimless, we took a bridge and some roundabout paths to avoid the roads and still-damp grasses, wearing, as we were, nothing on our feet but white plimsolls. My other items of clothing were a pair of pale green denim flares and a pink tie-dyed T-shirt. I opted to go hatless, as I considered my copycat Bolan corkscrewed hair protection enough from the sun. That was a mistake, I soon realised as the sun peaked, but there were many wooded areas to soothe my accidental bask with shadow.

I walked ahead of Jenny, swishing midges with my bottle of cider. The river wasn't yet visible, but I knew it was there, snaking south mile after mile, cinched in places to little more than a trickle between muddy banks and widening gloriously to surgent opulence in others. We could hear its gentle rush, sounding like a soft but urgent *shush* to all that was around it. We crossed a meadow to find it, following a line of bushes bankside that were like the thin shadows of rowers urging the river on.

It was a pure sight, and we stopped at the edge just to watch the swollen water take its course in brightness, serene transcendence trapped in every molecule that made it shine: the sun highlighting the muscles of the water's force so much I felt I was watching something that was fighting or clinging to the land for greater purchase to never be forgotten, almost as much as the memories I would later have.

I felt a punch in my side.

"Let's get moving, dreamboat," Jenny said, pointing further down the fields. "There's no place to picnic here."

I nodded, reluctantly breaking my visual bond with the river.

"I wonder how many have taken this way. Like the ancient followers, the firstlings of the land who took these footsteps and made these paths before anyone else. The history of a place is more than its names, you know," I bragged, treading softly behind her now, enraptured anew with the grace of her figure as she almost tiptoed through the grass.

"Just two less than are taking it now," she cast back at me while pulling the radio from her bag and turning it on, the station's crackle as caustic as a metal parrot, the dire reception as intermittent as the traffic we could just about hear from the nearby roads. I liked the quiet, but take away every sound and I find it unsettling. She switched off the radio, and I began tunelessly humming a song that had been stuck in my head for a while.

"Jai Guru Deva / Om / Nothing's gonna change my world ..." I couldn't remember all the words, and just repeated the refrain endlessly. It seemed to spill out of my head and fill the little silences between us as she walked ahead. I knew she didn't like Lennon, but it wasn't a goad: the song seemed naturally apposite, chiming with the atmosphere of the sweeping green land, the broad sunshine, the pulsing stream.

A slow hour of walking along untrodden paths, breezing through meadows, the occasional low of cows, the sudden fluting skirl of disturbed pheasants ... that's all it took to enter another world. We passed an odd little outbuilding with double archways set in the middle of nowhere, like a limestone dwarven fort: all turreted corners and stepped gables, the thinned remnants of a wood behind. I didn't like the place and hurried on, but I made a mental note that if the weather turned, here was shelter nearby. Seduced by the strong rhymical force of the river's ancient course, we walked on, unsure if we were being led or just following the sun, now higher and clearer, becoming the inconsiderate burden of the day.

As we wilted, we slowed down and sipped at the cider: it was warm. We saw a place on the riverbank that was scooped back, an overhanging grassy ledge giving it the appearance of a half-hammock. It was a good place to rest. Jenny scurried down, knelt into the river and plunged her bottle under the flow. In the haze it looked like she was drowning a cat. I followed and copied her. The banking grass was cool, the blades cold in the shadow, and we lay back supported by the earthen hammock, watching the Skerne slip past.

"What do you think the name means?" I said drowsily.

"What name?"

"Skerne."

Jenny shifted her gaze along the river, her thoughts as fossilised in the moment as a damselfly hung above the water.

"I think it means 'silver'. It's like a lost necklace in the grass."

"Nah, the twisted swarf of time itself!" I said, pulling the bottle from the water and taking a long glug. The cider was still warm.

"Very poetic," she said sarcastically, her muse instantly dead. "I'm tired; let's stay here, pet."

That pleasant and condensed moment of being together with her, being close, made my idea of following the river away to its end seem no more than brittle daydream. Cocooned against the bank, we could easily have slept there I felt, my eyes drifting off over the water and imagining the river for the next hundred miles, travelling as it's always travelled, resolute to its own course, some kind of truth. But Jenny stood and pulled me with her. Bag dropped, her hat flung off, the two bottles left in the water, we clambered back over the lip of the bank. I knew what she wanted, but before I lay down with her I scanned the distances keenly. All quiet, all serene, like an armistice. Safe enough, I supposed, and she was already on her back in the soft meadow grass. I knelt, just looking at her face as she looked at me. Her eyes were heavy-lidded, their hazel lustre dulled, her hair stroked behind her ears, her thin lips thickened with pout: it was the face of absolute desire. Her breathing was heavy, arching her form like all sexual tension unknotting at once. I only needed to unzip my jeans for her hands to grab at me and pull me into her. It was imperative, almost crude; her urgency was such that I rode it out feeling more passenger than driver. I never made a sound – but all her noises were deep-throated, a jolt to the earth as though her moans were digging her deeper into the grave of her own sudden death. It was always like this with her, a combination of *petit mal* and *petite mort*. She came and then came to almost immediately, her smile as though she'd re-entered the world from some celestial orbit. I think I loved her more in these moments than love could hold. But I was always wrong, for there was always more. Always. I lay beside her, and we slept.

* * *

What woke us was the tickle of drizzle on our faces. We rose quickly, the sky already darkening, and slipped down the bank to salvage the bag and our bottles with the unspoken intention of going back the way we'd come.

"Sugar!" Jenny spat, her usual euphemism for cursing. The bag was in the water, sunk, with a single handle grasping for the bank as though desperate for rescue; her hat was gone.

"Obviously the earth moved for you," I said with just the slightest leer.

"Tool."

But she was grinning as she pulled the bedraggled calico from the water. Tipping the contents out, we saw the ruined sandwiches flop on the bank like squashed jellyfish, the thin paper wrappers curdled with the salmon paste and cress. I suddenly felt very hungry seeing the ruined food, and reached for a swig from the bottle. At least the cider had cooled. Jenny shook water from her purse, rattling it like a tambourine, and passed it to me to tuck into my back pocket. The radio was dead, the petrified corpse of some little alien beast. I buried it underwater with a kick. Then, as if the day was suddenly over, the sky dulled, clouds like sullen concrete lumps blocked the sun and a fierce breeze flickered over the water, disturbing the surface with a million shivers. I shivered too – the river suddenly turned pewter with the petty hammering as though its sheen was being sprinkled with a slew of panel pins. We vaulted the bank hand in hand, saving only the cider, and we ran.

It wasn't a time to laugh, but there's something about running through rain that becomes a force in itself of human disregard, getting soaked becoming the equivalent of some weird rebirth of the soul, and it was this sense of wet joy that made me unable to control myself. So I laughed. I couldn't tell whether or not Jenny was laughing too, because by now the rain was battering us and my vision was hacked by the squall. All I felt was her hand tightening in mine as we ran, the blur of the old Gothic outhouse in the distance my only focal point. When we reached it we didn't hesitate to enter, although with the place languishing in such deep shadow we could have been jumping into a mine. Shaking our heads, pushing back our hair and wringing the rain from the strands, we stood just inside, a figure in each archway, like time had suddenly moulded us into the twin figures of an elaborate automaton clock stuck on the threshold of striking.

When we'd dried ourselves off best we could, we stood sombrely, assessing the situation. We were dressed for sun, not rain. We had no food, just two half-full bottles of cider, and we were miles from home with a hard, dispiriting storm battering the shelter. There was no hope of leaving just yet, so the decision to stay was forced upon us. The ground was dry inside the stone church-barn or whatever it was, the earth cooked hard by the long summer. I walked round it while Jenny stood mesmerised by the rain. In one corner was a flurry of little white-capped mushrooms, dozens of them sprouting around a big tree root that had broken under the stones and was now bulging upwards as if trying to lift the building on its own. I was hungry, but I wasn't sure if these were safe to eat.

Jenny joined me, saw me examining one of the little mushrooms I'd plucked and took it from me, pressing it against her nostrils. "It smells filthy," she said, inhaling deeply.

I took another one and smelled it. The rank, woody aroma suggested something both unearthly and sexual. I looked at her eyes and thought I saw her pupils dilated with pleasure, an odd purple tint to them in the dull light.

"Shall we eat them?" I asked uneasily.

"Only if we're starving," she said, petulantly throwing the pale little thing back into the shade.

"I *am* starving," I replied.

"Well, *you* eat them then, and if you collapse and die frothing at the mouth, I'll know not to bother."

She sounded annoyed with me. I guessed I was somehow being blamed for the rain. She walked back to the archway and stood, arms folded, leaning inside against the stone as if willing the rain to stop. I joined her and offered her a swig from my bottle. She drank from her own. Outside, the rain swept across the landscape like a painter with a rage-bristled brush destroying beauty that had been created long before. It wasn't cold, though. We steamed off our wetness easily in the muggy atmosphere, and were soon dry enough to hug, and then release the tension first by slow kisses, then the usual method: *venting the pent*, we called it.

Evening dropped itself upon us suddenly, the rain heavier, if anything, and we huddled in a corner near the dual archways, the dim light lying along the ground like a couple of coffins. We each had about a third of a bottle of cider left, and hadn't eaten since breakfast. I made a to-hell-with-it call, and went and plucked a handful of mushrooms from the ancient root. I carried them back, sat down and began nibbling at the cold edges of the fungi. The taste was somewhere between tangerine and onion, salted with earth and surprisingly lush with moisture. Jenny watched me in the gloaming ruin of the day – curious, I thought, to see if I keeled over. I didn't: the taste was pleasant, and, washed down with cider, began filling the great hole of my hunger.

"Have one," I offered.

As insouciantly as if she was accepting a fag in a nightclub, she took the smallest mushroom, broke off part of its cap and gently nibbled, her nervous fingers splitting the piece that was left into fine strands. She swallowed, took a swig of cider and seemed to relax immediately. I felt myself relax too. Then I began to hear the silences between the raindrops; they extended far beyond the time it should have taken till I heard the next sound.

This was the point – the exact point, when I look back – that time became a spontaneous distortion of itself, just for a microsecond, but enough for me to witness the mirrored unreality in everything around us.

* * *

Hunger, real hunger, makes you greedy. I ate enough of the mushrooms to satisfy my needs, but the more I ate the more I wanted. I cleared the clump by the old tree root, and despite the rain was all for going foraging into the wood behind the shelter had Jenny not pulled me back inside. I felt drunk – a feeling I couldn't fathom because the cider wasn't that potent, and it had been sipped slowly and sparingly over many hours.

Still it rained. We realised we had no option but to spend the night there, and lay down buddied up together as close to the wall as possible. I didn't think I would, but I slept, my last dozing thoughts a dream of walking away from here in the morning arm in arm with Jenny, the rain stopped, the fields clear and our memories blessed with a shared adventure.

But somewhere in the night I broke from the strange paralysis of a brutal nightmare, sweating and unsure of where I was. I wasn't with Jenny, that was certain. I was at the end of the shelter with the great tree root under its floor, my arms around its rotten girth as if I had been wrestling it in my sleep. I sat up. I could no longer hear the muffled hammer of rain upon the roof. Moonlight shone through the archways, delineating those coffins more sharply. I tried to stand but found I couldn't, my legs suddenly too fluid to form any resemblance to muscle and bone. I could hear something outside – a rhythmic series of pats and squeaks, as if someone was digging. Frustrated by my useless legs, I crawled forward, the floor like mulch in my fists, muddily foaming with my efforts like my own heartbeat attempting to break through my chest. It was dizzying, that short crawl, and I stopped several times before I got close enough to an archway and could see outside.

What I saw astonished me: *the river had moved*. I could see it sparkling even though it was laid under a rolling mist, and there was a frieze of figures moving through it, as if the river were a road. Hundreds of people, heads bowed, cowled, hunched ... a caravan of misery, it seemed. And then more resolute figures, proud, helmeted, shepherding the walkers. I stared and began to imagine them as legionaries, as if time had peeled back thousands of layers to present me with a mime played out a few yards from where I lay. I looked round again inside the shelter, and still I couldn't see Jenny.

I wanted to get up and test the dream by shouting and screaming, to tear through the fabric of its preposterous welter – but I couldn't rise. And then I saw her. *Jenny!* Out of the mists another sinister revelation brewed: she was laid on her back at the water's edge amidst a throng of bulrushes, and three of these mad, red-caped Brutuses were holding her down, one each on her arms, the third between her legs, thrusting himself backwards and forwards. I realised this was where the little squeaks emanated from: they were Jenny's plaintive yelps.

This spurred me to rise, and for a moment I stood unsteadily until something crushed me down again. I managed to turn my head and saw I was now underneath something like a massive equestrian statue, a faceless rider armed with sword and shield frozen mid-gallop, the stone steed rearing, flexing its left pastern like a mallet in a sling

And then, nothing. I was obliterated into dust.

● ● ●

When dawn broke and dream had fled, I woke up outside the shelter, my head splitting, my throat parched. Still, in some fury of sacrosanct disbelief at what I'd witnessed, I started to run up towards the river's edge, shouting Jenny's name. A still mist shrouded the water, infiltrating the fields beyond like the remnants of a fleeing army.

"What are you *doing*?" Jenny's voice rang out behind me.

When I turned she was on the threshold of the shelter, shielding her eyes. I gasped and walked back, shamefaced and confused.

"Where were you going?" she asked.

"Nowhere. I, I thought you'd gone. I thought I'd lost you," I babbled.

She looked at me keenly and put her hand to my head, turning my hair back over my ear with her finger comb.

"Where did you get that?"

I felt my temple and ran my finger over a rumple of ripped flesh. When I looked at my hand there was the rust of dry blood.

"I've no idea. I remember being outside during the night, and ..." I couldn't finish the sentence. Jenny pointed to a coping stone on the ground that had fallen off the roof in the storm. I just nodded dumbly.

Bending to inspect it, she found her purse half-buried beneath, the coins spilled on the ground like wet weld spatter. As she picked them up she turned one over in her palm and held it up for me to see. It was the smallest coin, a rough-edged silver *denarius* stamped one side with the noble face of a dateless emperor, the familiar penny Britannia on the reverse.

"How pretty," she said, enraptured by the find.

I shuddered, less pleased with the treasure. "Pretty odd, more like. Can we get on and go home," I moaned, "I've had enough of this place."

She took my hand like a child's as we walked across the fields, the miles going back seemingly much shorter than the miles coming here. The sun shone, my headache felt trivial, and we were happy again.

I was speechless about that nightmare, and remained so; wild mushrooms were also off the menu. But the main thing that tied our experience forever to this time and this river was what happened afterwards. Jenny became pregnant despite being on the pill, and nine months later gave birth to a son.

We called him Roman.

* * *

I never had the desire to go walking on the path beside that river again, and life soon carried us away on its own course, moving us south, further than the river ran, well away from the memory. Yet I never forgot.

Jenny, my wife for nearly fifty years, passed away a few weeks ago. But I have come back, and I am here now to lay at least two ghosts to rest, carrying her ashes under my arm as close to my heart as they can be cradled. I am knelt beside this ancient river to empty an obligation, serve an old memory its dues, not by burying her here, but by letting her ashes be taken on the wind to wherever the river wants to take her.

I hope it is a wonderful journey.

AUTHOR BIOGRAPHIES

Peter Barron is the former editor of *The Northern Echo*. He joined the paper as a reporter in 1984, and spent a year as editor of *The Hartlepool Mail* before rejoining *The Northern Echo* as editor in 1999. A former UK Columnist of the Year and one of the longest-serving editors in the regional press, he was awarded an MBE for services to journalism and community life in 2013. He now owns a media company specialising in writing, PR, presenting, broadcasting and after-dinner speaking. He is also a children's-book author. **www.peterbarronmedia.com**

Mark James Chappell lives and works in London. He graduated from Oxford University with a degree in Modern Languages before becoming a writer for film and television. "Tipster" is his first short story.

AUTHOR BIOGRAPHIES

Michael Drew was born and raised in West Cornforth, County Durham. He studied History and Creative Writing at university before leaving the UK to teach English as a foreign language. He currently lives in the south of Thailand.

Fran Edwards was born in Darlington and currently lives in Redcar. She was shortlisted for the Sid Chaplin short-story award (part of the Northern Writers' Awards), and has won a Scholastic Press children's-poetry competition. Her poetry has been published in anthologies by Iron Press and Black Light Engine Room Press, and by *Step Away* magazine. She is a member of Saltburn Writers.

Chris Lloyd is Chief Feature Writer of *The Northern Echo* and *Darlington & Stockton Times*, which are the regional and local newspapers respectively for the Brightwater area. He is a former North East Journalist of the Year, and as well as his analysis of local politics, he is known for his articles, books, talks and radio and TV broadcasts on local history.

AUTHOR BIOGRAPHIES

John Ridsdale was born 1953 in Pudsey, West Yorkshire. He left school aged fourteen and worked variously as an apprenticed sheet metal worker, welder, glover and antique book binder before spending nearly thirty years with Royal Mail. He moved to Newton Aycliffe in 2004. Now retired, he spends his free time pursuing lifelong interests such as writing, walking and playing chess.

Chrissie Robinson is a writer, playwright and poet, who has performed her poetry to audiences worldwide. "Gold Rush", her latest short story, was inspired by her participation on a creative writing course organised by Discover Brightwater and Paper + Ink. She lives in County Durham, where she is a community support worker.

Selected Titles from Paper + Ink

and the earth drank deep & Other Stories:
Winners of the Commonwealth Short Story Prize 2022

I Cleaned the – & Other Stories:
Winners of the Commonwealth Short Story Prize 2021

The Great Indian Tee and Snakes & Other Stories:
Winners of the Commonwealth Short Story Prize 2020

Emissaries: Stories and Reflections
Dean William Rudoy

In Dreams: The Very Short Works of Ryūnosuke Akutagawa
Selected and Translated from the Japanese by Ryan Choi

Million-Story City: The Undiscovered Writings of Marcus Preece
Edited by Malu Halasa and Aura Saxén

The Dead
James Joyce

The Overcoat
Nikolai Gogol
Translated from the Russian by Constance Garnett

Bartleby, the Scrivener
Herman Melville

Independence Day & Other Stories
Pramoedya Ananta Toer
Translated from the Indonesian by Willem Samuels

In the Shadow of Death
Rūdolfs Blaumanis
Translated from the Latvian by Uldis Balodis

www.paperand.ink